blue

blue

by m.k. brown

blue

ISBN (paperback): 979-8-234-01829-8

First Trade Paperback Original Edition, 2026

Printed in the United States of America

Cover Art by M. K. Brown, *Untitled*
Edited by Autumn Durand
Cover Design by Annie Cercone
Layout Design by Tiffany Quon and Krystle May Statler

for vanessa, anissa, and eric

CONTENTS

CREST

CRASH

for all the storms brewing in your heart

for all the love waiting for sunny days

for all the tears and prayers

for all those who go undiagnosed

for all those forced to bear witness

for all those who feel the sands of time

for all those swimming in resistance

for all those overwhelmed by our complex systems of othering

i hope you flow like water and heal the land

blue

climate change lullaby

climate change lullaby

i float through the sand

looking out to sea   i see

a mermaid   waiting for me

it sits on salty rocks   by the bay

cerulean sapphire skin on a yellow day

tendrils of seaweed for hair   nails of emerald   and shell

voice soft   clear   strong echo in a well

it calls to me:

come to the water's edge   then wade in deep

water from a dream of   soft   sleep

earth gives way to lemon heliotrope hues

they move

i am **h y p n o t i z e d** by the sway and bend of fin

the mermaid meets me at the sand bed's end

this   is   where   i belong   sea-funneled and—

i return to a world of disaster
i watch the mermaid dive, its tail following after
marching up a slope on the beach
to crusty parking lots, concrete filled with heat
my soles crack and boil
i step in tar and oil.

~~*concrete covered soil makes me sick~~
~~face paint, watercolors~~
~~all i see is the mermaid swaying over me~~
~~i wait for the rain, a lullaby~~
~~i have a home but home is not my mind*~~

rain to tears, sky to eyes

a drop falls in the ocean

standing

on the shore by the sea   eyes open

crystalline drops hit the surface

a gentle pour

puffy clouds with a purpose

i walk through the sand

feet   s   i   n k i   n   g   in

sediment   i waver   by the   water

looking   up and out   to   s e a   i see
an iridescent   hand

the creature   cries   to me:

come to the water's

edge

then wade in deep

tide of a time of dreamless sleep

the mermaid is farther

so i hold my
b
r
e
a
t
h and

swim

TROUGH

the unspeakable voyage

"the locals
know, there are things
in the water that would eat
you alive," but i cannot help but wade
through the shallows, searching for the
footsteps of my greatest
grandmother, lost

blue

sand raging dancing cats regretting
sleeping wilmington razors spitting wisps
rainclouds cement perry waiting pins
jacksonville numbers forgetting standing seagulls
late night choking los angeles spinning crashing
sharp teeth whiteville loving hating needles
heaving sweating working haunting new orleans
last song looking tobacco skin potomac
butcher sinking hunting salt counting
sheets little rock wrenching oak foam

sand mosquitoes pulse poison regretting
reaping wilmington whips fishing wisps
thimbles twine perry sicada nails
jacksonville rice betting sweeping seagulls
white bible choking los angeles yelling guitars
shadows whiteville loving stumbling claws

axes midnight working ghosts new orleans
strings sewing leather fire potomac
iron cotton hunting salt hiding
lying little rock running cedar foam

sand gurgling drowning bullets dying
raking wilmington granite writing bluebirds
stealing skulls perry listening dogs
jacksonville lights dreaming rusting ships
impaling tangerines los angeles matches breathing
carving whiteville loving warning whiskey
blood crocodiles swooning glass new orleans
blue moon watching fungus pulp potomac
cows seeping flesh salt gasoline
pepper little rock hoping oak foam

& then it's as if nothing ever happened at all

scorpion

my mother's mother once said
"romance without finance is a nuisance"
and she damn sho meant it
quick-talkin wit, no one was spared
she could sear a steak with a look
5 foot in height, 6 foot in presence
ardent storm, 1975 she cut & ran.

plutonic drums crack the undertow,
yoruba pulse against carolina ports

red in illinois
blue in california
but so, so true.

did you love me,
did you ever love me at all?

heart could not find beat
secret taken to grave.

if i go back, to the tomato vines
to the little white house in tennessee,
back to the long shadows of arkansas,
to the gullah geechee gospel,

if i listen closely

there was beauty in every valley of dying breath
"you could dance underwater and not get wet," scorpio.

when there was no music we weaved our own,
a 1500s sound that would carry the ages

she was carmen
she was grace
she was emma.

there is no grave big enough now,
are hymns the inheritance?

nimble sewing fingers
an eye for fashion
sharp mind.

searching for you in logs
folktales
myths

where did you find the breath?

how to live

in
order
to
live
on
land
where
nothing
fulfills

you
will
have
to
learn
how
to
grow
gills

divine as the bottom of the ocean

i.

mars yells at the underworld
poison blooms

pierces the eye
pierces the hand

a monarch butterfly
mythic the migratory paths that lead to ~~blue~~

grief grows three strange fruit
bloody crystal of time

divine as the bottom of the ocean

ii.

meadows of carnelian sunflowers
marigolds mar the sun

benevolent fire
collects ashes

falls in love
thinks about love

blind the warrior
tongue a spell

gods trade in narcissism
grief grows three strange fruit

screams of a silent broken thing

iii.

quiet forest
ancient soil

pulsing mercurial moods
azure sunlight upon river

heady mix of silver threads
puzzling with earth

catches stories from the air
carries a sheaf of wheat

& the griot's musings

why must i wake?

swift sickly swords burn down the sky
my body wakes and wonders why
i wish to think of lemon trees
i give myself up to soft seas

halfway here or there, cotton girl
i am a small deep-crusted pearl
age-old eastern sierra breeze
i give myself up to soft seas

nova-born death in september
pockets of what i remember
white-tailed rabbits, garden of ease
i give myself up to soft seas

meet me under a cancer moon
you are a kiss gone much too soon
marigolds grown over concrete
i give myself up to soft seas

corporate webs sticking to skin
vague futures, original sin
strange fruit dripping flesh, rotten leaves
i give myself up to soft seas

underwater manic circus spectacular

rape the culture
speak over the culture
have too much to say about the culture
politicize the culture
sensationalize the culture
tiktokify the culture
write papers about the culture
hand a latina a mic to rap about the culture
freestyle the culture
eat the culture
drink the culture
fuck the culture
laugh at the culture
mason jar the culture
bamboo earring the culture
host talk shows about the culture
ask the culture to come in through the back
remind the culture it's too black
remind the culture that it's too loud and aggressive
remind the culture what it can and cannot wear
devil's advocate the culture
liken the culture to another
jail the culture
disappear the culture
manipulate the culture
puppetshow the culture
vaudeville the culture
bribe the culture
police the culture
dehumanize the culture
coddle fragility around the culture
design cities to cage the culture
millions of bodies genocided for the culture
discarded in defiance protecting the culture

culture   lost   to   gravity   and   time

know nothing about the people who would've rather drowned
know nothing about the dances or the languages
know nothing about the land

do everything but remove colonial artifacts
do everything but defund the hands that pull triggers
do everything but pay healing reparations

much love and prayer
to the spirits
who carry the culture home

blood in the water

my greatest grandmother is dead
she closed her eyes and went to bed
she slowly sinks, her legs are lead
you'd think the sea was blue, but red

oh, the atlantic wind rejoiced
i hear she heard a gentle voice
it welcomed her with freedom's noise
so she made the ultimate choice

for carolina's rice gold coast
a ship sails on to loudly boast
the black daughters it hates the most
her soul swims free, so does her ghost

her story always contraband
but i promise i'll find the man
who dragged her from her mother's hand
soon he'll take <u>his</u> last breath on land

acidification

e x p o s i t i o n

a man texts me

wyd ?

r i s i n g a c t i o n

he thrusts

i yawn / i ask:

"may i trouble you with some marine ecology ? if you will sir– DO YOU KNOW ABOUT OCEAN ACIDIFICATION AND WHY IT IS ONE OF THE LARGEST ISSUES OF OUR TIME?"

he grunts

"no ? don't worry / it is an erotic tale ! / tiny tiny organisms called coral polyps make up a whole—a coral colony / these colonies collect to grow into a coral reef

he snarls

the polyps in these colonies use ions in seawater to secrete calcium carbonate to build an exoskeleton / the coral grows strong against the elements"

c l i m a x

he releases

much like james cook or adam smith or charles darwin or any other white-male-explorer-philosopher-scientist-economist who came all over the world / their seed rising high like carbon dioxide to the atmosphere

f a l l i n g a c t i o n

he spasms

i continue:

"loads of man-made carbon dioxide relentlessly released into the atmosphere wreak havoc on the biosphere / as above so below / changing the pH of the ocean / an infection on the ocean chemistry

he falters

coral polyps can no longer build exoskeletons / the symbiotic relationship between algae and polyps disrupts / entire ecosystems decay into wide vast dead things"

r e s o l u t i o n

he leaves

small [redacted], big [redacted]

a bat	a bomb	a book	a bill	a chain	a chain	a code
a cum	a dime	a dog	a fire	a fruit	a fright	a gang
a god	a gun	a hand	a hook	a hood	a hose	a hunt
a kiss	a knife	a law	a loan	a map	a mob	a noose
a pen	a rape	a rope	a rule	a ship	a sign	a slur
a song	a speech	a stare	a taunt	a tar	a word	a whip
a bank	a barn	a beach	a boat	a booth	a bus	a camp
a car	a chair	a church	a club	a cunt	a farm	a field
a floor	a grave	a gut	a heart	a home	a house	a jail
a lake	a land	a lung	a march	a meal	a pole	a pool
a scalp	a school	a show	a soil	a stage	a store	a street
a swamp	a town	a train	a tree	a womb	a wood	a wound

a dark and stormy night: act i

it was a dark and stormy night,
the wind sapphire in mad cyclones;
the onyx deep with murder's itch,
the moon glow blurred in tears and mist.

night's labyrinth cast long shadows,
the rust was singing in the breeze;
long after fish lines have slackened,
something terrible has happened.

"where is my baby?" the bluefin
tuna wailed, "did you see them go?"
"not i" the white-sided dolphin dived,
"not i" the sunflower star cried.

"nor i" crooned the hammerhead shark,
"nor i" waved the carnation tree;
"no" the brown algae slowly creeped,
"no" the salema sadly peeped.

in anguish then the bluefin sank,
"i know the way your inkling swam,"
the leatherback then softly spoke,
its whisper pale, a purple cloak.

a hush fell cold upon the seas,
the turtle neared in silent grace;
no sound but ghostly currents stirred,
no ripple broke its eerie word:

"there are long tales the slick has known,
of forever things, hard-shelled tomes;
we keep the magnet's solemn time,
i'll show you the scene of the crime."

FACE

synthetic blue

shiny blue reflections
bounce between buildings,
i am dizzied by the noise of cars,
the stink of street smells

sour like a poverty line on a tuesday
smells like small violence, step over the needy,
"sorry i have no change," *only credit cards*
i walk through oakland with discordant bursts of madness and guilt

i see the fibers of this year's blue nikes
blue lululemons draped over skin,
i see blue neon signs blinking open,
blue plastic bottles, blue wrappers

but i cannot see the sky

the mapmakers

"liberation is a spatial practice"
–mario gooden

slit soft wrists   wring out skin   milk fine hemoglobin
fall down
fall down
fall down
down
down
down

---

invisible creatures w r i t h e through maze-like muck
malnourished   sleepy   relentless

cement towers   ticking bombs   bloody bills

streets paved

streets paved

streets paved

paved

paved

paved

HAZARDOUS

definitely declining

red-yellow makers carve clocks in alien code

---

gulp coarse air

thick pulmonary constriction

steel cage

steel cage

steel cage

cage

cage

cage

clean air

the black birds sing of freedom

they say it is the best song they have ever sung

the deepest lapis stone they have ever seen

the warmest sunday sunrise they have ever felt

they say it is the widest horizon

i fear i will never know what the black birds do

swamp monsters in lake merritt

HELP! there are swamp monsters in lake merritt!
they almost pulled me in last night
dripping slosh of unknowable gunk, moss and mud
bacterial goop from another planet
filthy leftovers from another time

HELP! there are swamp monsters in lake merritt!
a cawed afternoon, a murder circles alpine trees
reflections beam over the water like a magnifying glass
do you ever wonder who is watching you?
ducks drift passively asleep, surveying the careless breeze
ever so often murders pile under a pale egg sky

HELP! there are swamp monsters in lake merritt!
people race past a folded blackened man
patagonia legs running toward some unseen finish line
i balance on the paved edge hoping never to go over

HELP! there are swamp monsters in lake merritt!
bubbling cauldron of lies and false folklore
well this is a very nice lake after all
it is quiet, except for the murder of course
shapeless, amorphous thing

HELP! i am trapped in the clutches of a swamp monster!
bogey creature stalks the shallows
boding forth stoic dreamers and outraged historians
waning sun sets over a transparent silver surface
i am sinking and i cannot see the bottom nor the beginning of its time

HELP! i am trapped in the clutches of a swamp monster!
fiendish, they eat any human who falls in

yank them at the root and steal their hair
grotesque, cigarette buds for eyebrows, grocery bags for lungs
they have an egalitarian society with a temple
and a library in the darkest part of the lake

HELP! i am trapped in the clutches of a swamp monster!
beady and ugly, they are gearing up for war
they use the egrets as spies to confer and plot their rise
the birds walk on water, through reeds inconspicuously

HELP! i am trapped in the clutches of a swamp monster!
through the struggle i wonder, what happens when the acid rises?
when the lake current carries debris?
the monster pulled me close and spoke a weathered language,
a drip-drip gargle gravelly echo

i looked into sunken eyes saturated with sight:
a wetland with a restaurant at one corner
a clothing store on the other
blackened people singing sweet
a white half moon
garlic grass
sparse
cawed
twigs
small flexible fruit
beige sand shore
madness under eucalyptus
palm trees and fairy lights
signs of the ohlone lost
saxophone and guitar picnics
friends and lovers laying on nasturtium
witches gathering rosemary and rosehip
cold crooked claws creaking to the sky
a scratching, pained gargle

one day i will see my swamp again

*i want to acknowledge and thank the ohlone people who have lived on this land for many, many years. their unceded territory extended from the bay area, down south to salinas valley. the sogorea te' land trust is an urban women-led land trust. they have a practice called the shuumi land tax, which asks folks who live here to pay the land tax in recognition of how we benefit from living on traditional ohlone land. the shuumi land tax is a practice in service of land back, and i encourage those who live in oakland to pay the land tax and for those who don't, to identify tangible ways to support land rematriation in your own communities.

microplastic daydreams

laminate me now i am a flat thing
i cannot escape dreaming in plastic
knock on my head   it would surely ring
pull at my sallow skin   it is surely elastic

i cannot escape dreaming in plastic
suture the hippocampus   massage the brain
pull at my sallow skin   it is surely elastic
please purchase better memories for this game

suture the hippocampus   massage the brain
elvis seared in my retina he picks at my heart
please purchase better memories for this game
rosy the reverie before tupperware   pray for a restart

elvis seared in my retina   he picks at my heart
when i wake up which dreams will i sing
rosy the reverie before tupperware   pray for a restart
laminate me   now   i am a flat thing

an evaporation of imaginary nothings

WHAT A
LIFE, HERE WE ARE
EXISTING, BUT NOT REALLY, SAY WHAT
YOU WANNA SAY, OR DON'T, YOU GO NOWHERE
IT'S RAINING, IT ALWAYS HAS, PEOPLE
ARE FINALLY STARTING TO
SEE IT
what a
life, here we are
existing, but not really, say what
you wanna say, or don't, you go nowhere
it's raining, it always has, people
are finally starting to
see it
what a
life here we are
existing but not really say what
you wanna say or dont you go nowhere
its raining it always has people
are finally starting to
see it

what a
life here we are
existing but not
really say what
you wanna say or don't you go
nowhere
its raining it always has
people
are finally
starting to
see it

wht

a

lyfe here we r

e x i s t i n g butt not rlly say
wht

u wanna say or dnt

u go nowhere

its rainin it alwys s has
ppl

r f i n a l l y startin to

s e a it

w

h

t a l y f e
r

e x i s
t

i

n g

b u
t
t

n
t
r l
ly s y
w

h

t

u
w ann a sa y or dn
t

u go knowhere

i t s r
a
in
i n
it h

as al wys
p pl

r f i n

a l l y s
ta

r t
i n
t
o

s e a i t

when am i enough?

to be forever drinking–
i learned thirst at 5 years old
i was never enough for me   sharp in the mouth   unsteady on my
own two legs   i'd drink for hours and hours   until my lungs were
exhausted   raspy   coarse   arid   thing of a girl

too far from the edge of the world

my bones decay   fine powder in the mortar and pestle

add two tablespoons of water and a dash of sugar

turn me into something palatable

gabapentin

"GENERAL ANXIETY DISORDER" the paper reads, a description for the heart tearing itself apart.

this is not visible on an ekg, a threat almost imaginary but just as lethal. i feel that pressure on my chest like tons of particulate matter pressing on my lungs.

gravity splits me open.

"YOU NEED TO BREATHE & SMILE MORE" the asian, male doctor tells me as he prescribes me nothing.

i would later move 300 miles away to a different city with a rich black history of justice, truth, & civil disobedience.

folks who traded in their lives for their neighbors, to a place where a black psychiatrist finally prescribes me gabapentin.

"100MG TWICE A DAY IF NEEDED"

a non-addictive medication used to prevent & control seizures.

also used to relieve nerve pain.

also, off-label, used to calm the symptoms of anxiety.

"TEXAS RIVER RISES IN 45 MINUTES WITH A DEATH TOLL OF AT LEAST 100 INCLUDING CHILDREN" gabapentin "THE BIG UGLY BILL PASSES OUT OF THE SENATE & THE HOUSE INCLUDING VOTES FROM 8 CALIFORNIA POLITICIANS, TO LEAVE THOUSANDS WITHOUT HEALTHCARE" gabapentin

who knew that a little white capsule could help the lungs do what
they were always meant to?

breath is as ancient as human & storytelling.

so tell me why i cannot breathe?
i.cannot.breathe.

i cannot breathe when thousands of children & adults are made
to dig for lithium with their bare hands for pennies a day.

i cannot eat when i watch israel drop bombs & bullets bought
with my own tax money.

i cannot think as i scroll across my phone just to see another
white officer murder a black person.

i cannot sleep knowing a simple traffic stop can lead to years
trapped within the prison-industrial slavery system.

i can pinpoint the imaginary holes in my heart as the cortisol
seeps in.

so
i
take
my
gabapentin.

& i draw my curtains, & i am quiet.

i write, i cry, i hold my cats.
i call my friends.

i do what i can today, though my chest constricts,
so i don't leave this world with a wasted breath.

where are the bodies?

under the bombs under the bombs under the bombs
under the gun under the gun under the gun
under the fire under the fire under the fire

---

under the cracks under the cracks under the cracks
under the rubble under the rubble under the rubble
under the ashes under the ashes under the ashes

---

under the limbs under the limbs under the limbs
under the skin under the skin under the skin
under the soil under the soil under the soil

---

under the prayer under the prayer under the prayer
under the song under the song under the song
under the tears under the tears under the tears

---

and now

under

the sea

resist

| my | bedsheets | doused | in | salt | water |
| nightmare | teardrops | trickle |

| down |

| down |

| down |

to	my	hands
i	collect	droplets
in	my	pockets
to	a	protest
to my friends

what happens after?

only god knows   when i will sleep soundly

the world keeps me awake

how can so much movement amount to nothing

move in circles

only god knows   when the tears will stop

how the story ends

there is nothing in my brain

i feel stupid

only god knows   when it will be enough

how many children swept away by a bloody river

floating downstream

counting warplanes in their dreams

only god knows   what happens after there is nothing left to burn

left to flood

circling a drain

only god knows when the stars will fall

when this world will collapse

fill with dust

turn inside out

only god knows what's in the next dimension

what's in the next life

—will you go with me?

where are the bodies? pt.ii

ler the bombs under the bombs under
bombs under the gun under the gun
ler the gun under the fire under the
: under the fire under the bombs
ler the bombs under the bombs under
gun under the gun under the gun
ler the fire under the fire under the
:

---

ler the cracks under the cracks
ler the cracks under the rubble under
rubble under the rubble under the
es under the ashes under the ashes
ler the cracks under the cracks
ler the cracks under the rubble under
rubble under the rubble under the
es under the ashes under the ashes

---

ler the limbs under the limbs under
limbs under the skin under the skin
ler the skin under the soil under the
under the soil under the limbs under
limbs under the limbs under the skin
ler the skin under the skin under the
under the soil under the soil

---

ler the prayer under the prayer under
prayerunder the song under the
g under the song under the tears
ler the tears under the tears under
prayer under the prayer under the
yerunder the song under the song
ler the song under the tears under
tears under the tears

under the bombs under the bombs under
the bombs under the gun under the gun
under the gun under the fire under the
fire under the fire under the bombs
under the bombs under the bombs under
the gun under the gun under the gun
under the fire under the fire under the
fire

---

under the cracks under the cracks under
the cracks under the rubble under the
rubble under the rubble under the ashes
under the ashes under the ashes under
the cracks under the cracks under the
cracks under the rubble under the rubble
under the rubble under the ashes under
the ashes under the ashes

---

under the limbs under the limbs under
the limbs under the skin under the skin
under the skin under the soil under the
soil under the soil under the limbs under
the limbs under the limbs under the skin
under the skin under the skin under the
soil under the soil under the soil

---

under the prayer under the prayer under
the prayerunder the song under the song
under the song under the tears under the
tears under the tears under the prayer
under the prayer under the prayerunder
the song under the song under the song
under the tears under the tears under the
tears

under the bombs under the bombs under
the bombs under the gun under the gun
under the gun under the fire under the
fire under the fire under the bombs
under the bombs under the bombs under
the gun under the gun under the gun
under the fire under the fire under the
fire

under the cracks under the cracks
under the cracks under the rubble under
the rubble under the rubble under the
ashes under the ashes under the ashes
under the cracks under the cracks
under the cracks under the rubble under
the rubble under the rubble under the
ashes under the ashes under the ashes

under the limbs under the limbs under
the limbs under the skin under the skin
under the skin under the soil under the
soil under the soil under the limbs under
the limbs under the limbs under the skin
under the skin under the skin under the
soil under the soil under the soil

under the prayer under the prayer under
the prayer under the song under the
song under the song under the tears
under the tears under the tears under
the prayer under the prayer under the
prayer under the song under the song
under the song under the tears under
the tears under the tears

teach us how to start again

under the bombs under the bombs un
the bombs under the gun under the g
under the gun under the fire under t
fire under the fire under the bombs
under the bombs under the bombs un
the gun under the gun under the gun
under the fire under the fire under th
fire

under the cracks under the cracks u
the cracks under the rubble under th
rubble under the rubble under the as
under the ashes under the ashes unde
the cracks under the cracks under th
cracks under the rubble under the ru
under the rubble under the ashes und
the ashes under the ashes

under the limbs under the limbs und
the limbs under the skin under the sk
under the skin under the soil under t
soil under the soil under the limbs u
the limbs under the limbs under the
under the skin under the skin under
soil under the soil under the soil

under the prayer under the prayer u
the prayer under the song under the
song under the song under the tears
under the tears under the tears under
prayer under the prayer under the pr
under the song under the song under
the song under the tears under the te
under the tears

a dark and stormy night: act ii

it was a dark and stormy night,
the hulls did moan against the wind;
the iron scratched at murder's itch,
the moon sung pale through tears and mist.

"we must find now a brutal sort,"
the leatherback in murmurs said;
"its many faces will know where,
your baby went in this nightmare."

away the turtle cut the waves,
towards deepwater horizon;
on paths of steel and disaster,
the bluefin tuna swam after.

then down they went past trawling nets,
through frenzied rust and broken sleep;
past slickened stones and marrowed bone,
under a place of rot alone.

a many-headed monster sat,
beneath the drill where poison blew;
its heads rose out from silt and crud,
proud with pearlescent sheen and blood.

"my baby–where?" the tuna urged,
but only laughed the beast instead;
IF YOU MUST ASK THEN YOU WILL KNOW,
MY PURPOSE IS TO GROW AND GROW.

YOUR PURPOSE IS TO FEED THE FLAME,
TO FILL THE BELLY OF A BEAST,
TO KISS THE LINES THE EMPIRE THROWS,
AND SATE THE GREED THAT NEVER SLOWS.

“why such horrors?” the tuna cried,
“the inkling—tell me, where it goes,”
the turtle roared, “you sickly beast!”
yet begged within its heart for peace.

YOUR BABY IS DEAD, the beast hissed,
NOW OIL AND FLESH AND SURFACE KISSED;
IN SCARLET SLICK THAT MOCKS THE RAIN–

AND SOON YOUR FATE WILL BE THE SAME.

THE MANY-HEADED MONSTER

BIG OIL

EXXONMOBIL
SHELL
BP
CHEVRON
TOTALENERGIES
CONOCOPHILLIPS
VALERO ENERGY
PHILLIPS 66
EOG RESOURCES
CHENIERE
PIONEER NATURAL RESOURCES
OCCIDENTAL PETROLEUM
DIAMONDBACK ENERGY
MARATHON OIL
HESS

BIG WEALTH / BIG TECH / BIG CORP

BLACKROCK
VANGUARD
STATE STREET
BERKSHIRE HATHAWAY
BLOOMBERG LP
JPMORGAN CHASE
BANK OF AMERICA
WELLS FARGO
GOLDMAN SACHS
CITIBANK
U.S. BANK
CAPITAL ONE
TD BANK
PNC BANK
TRUIST BANK
AMAZON
GOOGLE
MICROSOFT
APPLE
META
ORACLE
TESLA
WALMART
FOXCONN
G4S

BIG PLASTIC

DOW CHEMICAL CO.

BIG POLICY

U.S. PRESIDENT
U.S. VICE PRESIDENT
U.S. CABINET
U.S. SENATORS
FEDERAL BUREAU OF PRISONS

BIG ENERGY

SEMPRA
PG&E CORPORATION
NEXTERA ENERGY INC.
DOMINION ENERGY
THE SOUTHERN COMPANY
DUKE ENERGY CORPORATION

BIG FOOD

UNILEVER
DANONE
MARS
MONDELEZ
ASSOCIATED BRITISH FOODS
MITSUBISHI CORPORATION
KELLOG'S
PEPSICO
NESTLE
COCA COLA
GENERAL MILLS
MARUBENI CORPORATION

BIG PHARMA

PFIZER
JOHNSON & JOHNSON
ABBOTT
MERCK & CO
STRYKER
REGENERATION PHARAMCEUTICALS
BRISTOL-MYERS SQUIBB
ABBVIE
ELI LILLY AND COMPANY

BIG PESTICIDES / BIG SEEDS

CHEMCHINA
LIMAGRAIN
BAYER
SYNGENTA AG
CORTEVA (DOW AND DUPONT) AGROSCIENCES
BASF
MONSANTO

AND MANY MORE...

boycott

divest

sanction

CREST

a call from destiny

someone once said *"for black people the past is painful, the present is precarious, but the future is free"*
i am telling you now:

pick up your picket sign, your power is guaranteed

in the center of your chest, your heart beats to one chord,
a distant sound wave carried from outer space, or a force pulling your matter towards mine

watch as plastic towers pushing towards the sky melt-burn-tumble

wrap your hands around community
grow love like tomatoes in a side garden

grow love like it's your last day to breathe

prepare for blast off, we are skipping stones to new realities
follow radiant stars pointing north to pluto as it transits aquarius

dwarf planet, craterous and mountainous

stark with renewal
shed this skin, this life, crusty and dry

pick at pustules boiling over with nuclear brimstone and hatred

bleed these wounds until there are no wars,
no soot falling, microscopic destruction of the lungs

every part of your body is star-kissed

we are from the same luminous black implosion, a cloud of solar gas and dust
we are vibrating in pools of light and shadow together

our trees we planted 54 years ago, roots singing for revolution

reaching, reaching for tectonic movement they cannot yet touch
unearthing that towers are built on shifting sand not lithospheric rock

the only thing guaranteed is our future

i am here from that distant infinite
to tell you that we win, come hell or highwater

we win

as long as you keep your head to the sky
we win

dreaming in our collective spell for change

folkloric spark to remember: your existence is pure
pure joy, starlight on the deepest night

dust from another plane

born again, and again
election after election

dictator after dictator

misery crumbles, giants do die
the bigger they are, the harder they fall

what is loosed in the heavens

will be loosed on earth
in the great come down heaven has always had your name

but if you cannot settle for distant constellations

look around, heaven is an old growth forest
leaves whispering age-hardened secrets

look around, heaven is electromagnetic force

the magic of what we can't see
look around, heaven is a walk with a friend

pearlescent affirmations for your existence here and now

pick up your picket sign, your power is guaranteed
yes, the past is painful, the present is precarious, but the future is
free

2 : 22

a tender thing   you and me
meandering to higher ground
          riparian irises bloom on our edge for miles
you collect waterborne agate and jasper just for me
            i keep them on my dresser
you write letters about my curls and all our past lives
 this is our twelfth time
            but our unfolding is always a surprise
the current caresses my inner thighs   the soft pull whispers to
all the soft places you've kissed

there is no despair to see how we transform from turquoise
     to emerald
                    i hold my ear beneath the surface to listen
the sound of us   chords   infinite   flow
variation
                    the magic of perilous rapids on the cusp of
drowning
                                        but we always dream
we always change and we come up as ourselves
                         there is a destination but we rarely think of it

               glass surface carving heavy through an ancient history
                    the last in the season of aquarius
                         rock as the clock face

          you keep count in riverian time

a drop to soothe the nerves

1. a glittering of sea otter tears for grief
2. one part chamomile / one part beer flower

   to get you back to sleep
3. heavy blankets to cocoon your chill
4. 1000 milligrams of ibuprofen to mute
5. 3 gratitudes on the lips
6. 3 releases on the flame
7. dandelion for wishes
8. lavender to absolve guilt and shame
9. a sprinkling of seaweed
10. fresh driftwood on the altar
11. blue lotus for intuition
12. 3 basil leaves in the pot
13. a penny for the ancestors
14. red jasper in your pocket

a very gray day

quakes

on

the

inside

she

smiles

on

the

outside

clip

clop

beats

pump

she

sees

nothing

sees

gray

grips
pulls
shakes
suffocates

new moon in cancer

what life is this cancer?
i count the seasons back to you

close to the earth, crunching of soil
you are a soft home to me

you teach me to be gentle with myself
believe in the wet flesh in the middle of my chest

you are a realm of blue
a small caress, a sigh of the sea in a lost dream

i hear the call of my deepest cry– a song of black and white pictures

chain link fence where grass grows like shattered jade
and tiny violet wildflowers sprout in full
no name, no rules

parakeets in the neighbor's giant lemon tree
marking the hour, confusing the time

chile pepper bushes
blooms of heat and tang on my tongue

i am alone in 27 years

i wait for you under a rock, in a shell
27 years come virgo

i may be older and sometimes wiser, each year a storybook unto itself
chapters full of fables-villains-mishaps-misfortunes-happy endings

warm is your call to me, sensual notes of prayer
quiet murmurs to being

a bath-like reminder that things will always be dirty
but i have a home to soak my skin clean

message in a bottle

march 25, 2024

shuffling through san francisco's ocean beach
on a cloudy afternoon, combing the shore for sand dollars

the wet dogs are flying fish in the pacific waves

i make my way close to the icy tide's edge and almost miss
the weathered glass bottle that washes up at my brown feet

inside the bottle a slip of parchment reads:

"bring me all of your dreams,
you dreamers.
bring me all of your
heart melodies
that i may wrap them
in a blue cloud-cloth
away from the too rough fingers
of the world."
–langston hughes

celestial gratitude crashes and ricochets through my bones
for the black people who make dream-work their reality

who scour the earth for missing maps, or piece together new ones

for the black people who magnetize their compasses to navigate
precarious waters as courageous acts of care for their community:

hazel m. johnson
robert bullard
erika huggins
john huggins

dorceta taylor
dianne d. glave
carolyn finney
andre baptiste
alexis nikole
james baldwin
emma dupree
bell hooks
sharon lavigne
angela davis
kathleen cleaver
huey p. newton
tamika butler
rose brewer
robin d. g. kelley
kimberlé crenshaw
keeanga-yamahtta taylor
shirley chisholm
shalanda baker
octavia butler
mikki kendall
ron finley
leah thomas
marcus anthony hunter
zandria f. robinson
frantz fanon
audre lorde
phillis wheatley
aniya butler
toni morrison
bunchy carter
stokely carmichael
bobby seale
fred hampton
mark clark
assata shakur
john francis
ira wallace
tyrone hayes
warren washington
marsha p. johnson
adrienne maree brown
ladonna redmond
sedrick brown
sletsy dlamini
ashia ajani
joycelyn longdon
aminah luqman
ashley myrriah
vivian breckenridge
mercedes gibson
ashly loibman
mikayla tillery
hannah rowntree
lilly amechi
dakoury godo-solo
inonge mubita
kalina browne
larissa johnson
carolin tolentino

alice walker
ntozake shange
mari copeny
wawa gatheru
patricia smith
breonna jones
jacqueline patterson
jerome foster ii
gina dent
beth e. ritchie
ruth wilson gilmore
heather mcteer toney
ella baker
colette pichon battle
barbara ransby
gwendolyn brooks
evie shockley
william darity
a. kirsten mullen
lucas hubbard
mary annaïse heglar
mariame kaba
christopher paul harris
james metoyer
taren evans
jona davis
anjeanette brown
dorothy roberts
cyree jarelle johnson
cheyney mcknight
ayana elizabeth johnson
tiffani ashley bell
kahlil greene
melanie l. harris
roishetta ozane
lucille clifton
mary hook
thérèse cator
beverly wright
jamiah e. hargins
catherine coleman flowers
deseree fontenot
camille dungy
maurissa brown
hiram sims
camari hawkins

and so many, many more...

always

keep the hope alive
capillaries unblocked
do not wait to exhale

let the blood in your chest flow
let your voice ride the air to new life
let your pen ink blue-green worlds beyond this one

when your chest starts to fatigue and tighten
when your words start to quiver
do not give in

your breath is protected by many black moons
black suns and silver stars
they are with you

always

today

this world is just a collision of things
atoms collide vibrate sing

silliness violence unpredictable impact
yellow red orange violet teal

take one breath
then another:

i hope your heart feels full today
love your body

feel purpose
wiggle your toes

i hope you chase nonexistent dreams today
dance love be soft

i hope you feel seen today
let go of sharpness

stand still
laugh be endless

i hope the trees sway just for you today
cry then cry some more

i hope you wander the streets today
know peace be broken that's okay

lost but time finds you

i hope you dance naked under the moon

oh, what a magic woman, she
walks to the sound of her own heartbeat,
uses words that fit the puzzles in her mind
but no one else's

oh, what a magic woman, she
bathes in oils to heal her skin,
rinses with water to heal her soul,

her side tables and shelves are lined with creams and lotions,
perfumes and potions, spellbooks and reading books,
herbs and medicines,
she could make a love spell...or a really great face mask

oh, what a magic woman, she
dances fully clothed under full light,
strips to analyze her body naked,
rejoices to find beauty where she assumed there was none

oh, what a magic woman, she
knows the power of her own thighs,
they hold her form to the sky
even when she feels she'll never reach it

coordinates back to los angeles & oakland

paradise smells
like seasoning
salt on three dollar
french fries

the ghettobird on
42nd street *sings*
who do ya luv r u 4 sure
i never knew there was a
love like this before
i wonder if heaven's got a ghetto

it can't because heaven is an old growth
forest juicy apple from a tree directly into
the palm today was a good day where is huey where is
angela they are thinking of systematic change for collective
liberation and if u stay ready u aint got to get ready

can you imagine

paradise
looks like
permacultured
frontyards
surrounded by
deep rooted

perennials
love never knew
what i was missin
but as soon as we
begin to resist the
urge to consume
and be consumed
there will be no
othering
just belonging

it's all local from the river to
sea our people's land is free
always remember earth's future
needs black memory we are
blue but we are a lot of other
colors too little black babies in the sky
as silver stars follow their coos 37
degrees north from 90224 to 90037 to
the 94612 past the 110 past the 5 past the 580 past the
880 until you hear turn my music up my shit bang

CRASH

glass and steel

canyon cities

stars have secrets

i have decades of red

rage to process it's been

raining too long too young

to be this hurt i have questions

parking lot blues heaven's got a

plan for you i think we teach girls to

shrink themselves i wonder if whales have dreams too hopscotch through time it was a murder and a crime who needs a heart if a heart can be broken and the pieces sold separately

inside us there is everything loving would be easy if your colors were like my

dreams karma is
a bitch but she's a
beautiful thing often
i don't want the thing
i want the way the
thing makes me feel
rap is the same as
shakespeare except less
privilege what if the sky and
the stars are for show and the

aliens are watching live waiting to

die in this artificial world we've built

curated picture of a life if i

told you that a flower bloomed in a

dark room would you trust me

heartbreak is like breathing but healing

is too w i n d ***sound** and color the

song of an uprising now calls the mother flying

above the city lights i love when the clouds look like

trees my country 'tis of thee sweet land of liberty how is it

that i was good then i was bad then i was nothing

down in the river to pray

as i go down in the river to pray
studyin' about that ole good way
i walked backwards twice today
to see sallow swans sing and sway

i watched a kingfisher hunt its prey
dive in a blur of blue and gray
fish guts and bloody scales on display
current humming sweetly as it floats away

as i go down in the river to pray
studyin' about that ole good way
i met a tall man with a lot to say
he did not go down in the river to pray

by and by i still go 'round and lay
studyin' about that ole good way
sycamore hung destitute with decay
as i go down in the river to pray

remember you are loved

UNTIL THE ROCK CRACKS OPEN
UNTIL THE RED HAWK DIES
UNTIL THE YAMS ARE MASHED
UNTIL THE RIVER WIND IS DONE
UNTIL THE SUN ENDS ITS TURN
UNTIL THE YELLOW HAY BURNS
UNTIL THE OKRA IS TENDER
UNTIL THE WAVE ENDS IT BREAK
UNTIL THE WILLOW STOPS WEEPING
UNTIL THE THUNDER IS QUIET
UNTIL THE LIGHTNING CALLS
AS BIG AS THE SKY
AS DEEP AS THE MARIANA
AS OLD AS THE SEQUOIA
AS LONG AS A BLADE OF GRASS
AS INTRICATE AS LIMESTONE
AS STRONG AS THE WHALE SINGS
AS SOUND AS THE BEAR SLEEPS
AS STUBBORN AS THE SEAGULL
AS TRUE AS THE CICADA CRIES
AS LONG AS THE MOJAVE IS DRY
AS WARM AS THE CARIBBEAN WATERS

YOU ARE LOVED
YOU ARE LOVED
YOU ARE LOVED

a garden is a portal

my great-grandfather grew tomatoes, greens, and blackberries on a small plot of land in chicago. i know this because my mother told me. my mother is a keeper of time, a teacher, luminous and brilliant. feet to soil, he grew sovereignty for his family, a sharecropper's dream. my mother smiles when she talks about him. i have held my hands to soil many times. from baldwin hills to berkeley i chased butterflies towards the sun and felt dazzled by the rain. i felt for the softness of garlic stems to pluck from velvet earth. i didn't know i was walking the streets searching for plots to tend. my ancestors talk to me through the soil. i feel them waving at gates to gardens. they speak broken english to me when i sleep. i forget the words when i wake. but i find sentences rushing back to me as i pull deep weeds and carve dirt holes with my fingernails. tomatoes speak in an orange tangy tongue. juicy with flesh, a simple bite brings daydreams of summers i barely remember, tells me stories about my great-grandfather's job at the post office, his favorite routes to walk. the collard greens murmur tender, earthy tales about my great-grandmother's plush hands and sharp mouth as she made home for children, then later became a nurse. a spicy pungence stains their love story in the corners of my brain. they had to work their whole lives. i cannot ask them what brought them breath, that small elusive seed. i collect any seeds i find, sorting for histories i hope to save and later interpret for a map back to the midwest. thank the divine my family's dreams were never lost, only planted. transmuted through soil and water, tended by ticking clocks and sleepless nights devoted to something more, that sweet far thing. my mother walks a few steps farther than her mother, trailing oval-shaped blackberries seeds so i know alchemy too. i do not know all the different hues and spells for planting, but at least i know the direction.

navigating a lost ship: assata shakur was right

i believe in my mother's glowing smile,
my brother's infectious laugh

pennied afternoons,
pink rolling hills

i believe in blaring music,
late night calls and midnight drives

whispering spells to constellations,
shooting stars

i believe in bedtime stories,
waking up without clocks

slow mornings,
lovers holding hands

i believe in the healing hum of cat purrs,
quiet sunday cuddles

rereading favorite books,
singing with friends

i believe in the good in people,
small moments and long hugs

golden rays of warm days,
foggy winter rain

i believe in kissing wounds,
catching dawn

the fullness of every life,
brash odes to being

i believe our bodies will return,
rich earth to feed flowers

i believe in blue
i believe in you

i believe in being sad for awhile if i have to but–
i believe in living too.

notes

"the unspeakable voyage" references a quote "the locals know, there are things in the water that would eat you alive" from the book *the house of rust* written by khadija abdalla bajaber.

"the unspeakable voyage" is an eintou. the eintou was invented by cosima smith.

"scorpion" references a quote "you could dance underwater and not get wet," from evie shokley's poem "pantoum: landing, 1976"

"why must i wake" is a kyrielle.

"blood in the water" is written in iambic tetrameter, contains 8 syllables in each line, and 16 lines.

"a dark and stormy night" acts i and ii contain 8 syllables in each line.

"the mapmakers" references a quote "liberation is a spatial practice" from *dark space: architecture, representation, black identity*, a collection of essays by mario gooden.

"an evaporation of imaginary nothings" is an eintou that evaporates into a jumble of nothings.

"microplastic daydreams" is a pantoum.

boycott, divest[ment], sanction or BDS is a movement that has helped intensify campaigns for justice. inspired by south africa's anti-apartheid movement, the BDS movement is a palestinian-led movement for freedom, justice, and equality that has gained international support.

"a call from destiny" was published (2024) in an online issue, *shaping destiny: election season, before, during and after, in about place journal*, a literary journal created by the black earth institute dedicated to re-forging the links between art and spirit, earth and society.

"a call from destiny" references a quote "for black people the past is painful, the present is precarious, but the future is free." this quote was popularized by erika alexander, an iconic actress, writer, producer, and activist.

"message in a bottle" references the poem "the dream-keepers" by langston hughes.

"coordinates back to los angeles & oakland" features lines from songs: "who do ya luv r u 4 sure" loungin (who da ya luv) by ll cool j; "i never knew there was a love like this before" love like this by faith evans; "i wonder if heaven's got a ghetto" i wonder if heaven got a ghetto by 2pac; "today was a good day" it was a good day by ice cube; "love never knew what i was missin" love by keyshia cole; "turn my music up my shit bang" my shit bang by e-40.

"coordinates back to los angeles & oakland" references "no othering just belonging" a concept i came across from the othering & belonging institute in berkeley. the institute studies systems and processes of exclusion, and aims to build a world where all belong.

"coordinates back to los angeles & oakland" references the idea "systematic change for collective liberation," an idea drawn from the cycle of liberation.

"coordinates back to los angeles & oakland" features a quote "from river to sea our people's land is free" that i edited under inspiration from the freedom protest call "from the river to sea, palestine will be free."

"picking up the pieces" uses many notable songs and phrases drawn from media like i have questions by camila cabello; don't you worry child by swedish house mafia; we should all be feminists by chimamanda ngozi adichie; what's love got to do with it by tina turner; karma chameleon by culture club; pink matter by frank ocean and andre 3000; poetic justice by kendrick lamar; my country, 'tis of thee by samuel francis smith.

"down in the river" is inspired by a negro spiritual, the good old way.

"navigating a lost ship: assata shakur was right" is an ode to the poem "affirmation" by assata shakur.

acknowledgments

since i was a child, i've always wanted to become a published author, and i'm in complete awe of my journey here to this moment.

thank you to camari carter hawkins and mama's kitchen press for your partnership, support, and encouragement! we need more small presses like yours in the world, thank you for believing in me and my work.

thank you to autumn durand and anne marie for your editorial guidance.

thank you to annie cercone for taking a piece of artwork i painted in 2020, during the haze of uncertainty of the pandemic, and turning it into something wonderful: the cover of this book. i'm so grateful for your design eye.

thank you to tiffany quon for your attention to detail, patience, and ability to design my ideas into being. i appreciated your compassion and dedication.

thank you to krystle may statler–you are a star. your interior and exterior design support has meant the world, and i'm so proud of what we've created. from my scribbles to charts, you tackled it all.

thank you to my sunday evening community literature initiative cohort led by the wonderfully talented margaret garcia and crystal reyes. our time together was always the highlight of my week, and i cannot express enough gratitude. thank you to my entire cohort for all the encouragement and support.

thank you to the community literature initiative team and managers. y'all are amazing!

thank you to evie shockley, langston hughes, khadija abdalla bajaber, and the many great storytellers before me.

thank you to my high school english teachers jacqueline barrios, kate mcfadden, and myra lebendig, as well as one of the most magical librarians i've ever met, benin lemus. there was never a dull moment for me when it came to reading literature during such a crucial developmental period in my life, because i was surrounded by kick ass, witty women who had such a passion to share.

thank you to hiram sims for being my high school poetry teacher and taking your time to show up to saturday school and share the gospel of writing poetry (and dope rap music). your impact on my life has been immeasurable.

thank you to my mother for imbuing me with the power of storytelling, a deep love of reading, and a strong sense of service to my community. i had the privilege to sit in your classroom at a young age with hundreds of books within my reach and hours to read. i have always been inspired by your devotion to your community. thank you for gifting me a shiny gold journal and sparkly pens for christmas when i was seven years old. i learned i loved to write that day, and that it was important to take intentional time to do so. i still have that journal (not the pens unfortunately), but that journal evolved into many more journals, and eventually led me to poetry.

and lastly, to the reader, thank you for your support. i hope you find words you can carry with you, always.

about the author

maurissa brown (she | her) is a neurodivergent poet, artist, environmental justice advocate, and climate equity policy professional born and raised in south central los angeles, california. currently based in oakland, she works to shift decision-making power to low-income communities and communities historically impacted by redlining, to protect these very folks from climate change. she earned a bachelor of science in ecology, behavior, and evolution, with a minor in theater from the university of california, los angeles. her poetry has appeared in *about place* journal and *seventh wave* magazine.

blue is a collection of poems inspired by the depths of the ocean and other bodies of water. maurissa invites the reader to wade through the wave-like journey of sadness, grief, rage, love, disillusionment, and hope that accompanies the loss of a healthy planet, loss of place and future. maurissa's poems explore what it feels like to live in a society that values violence above all. her voice sets the stage to remember a dark past, struggle with the present, and wonder about the future in hopes of finding resilience, community, and love under the pressures of time.

you can find her at mkbrownwriter.com.

Made in the USA
Coppell, TX
14 June 2026

409512R10066